How to get clients for your business

Shonda Miles

Copyright

Copyright © 2016 Shonda Miles

For more information on Shonda Miles, go to www.shondamiles.com. Shonda Miles offers a range of Products and Services including Multiple Streams of Income-how to make money while you sleep and How to make an extra $100,000 this year.

10 Ways to Write an EBook every 10 days
101 Success Questions that will change your life
Remote Medical Coding Jobs
Tips for Staring an Online Business
How to Love Your Spouse again
How to Double Your Income in 12 Months or less
50 Tips to Jumpstart Your Success
50 Streams of Income
How to Get the Job You Want
21 Ways to Start a Marriage off Right
18 Ways to Break into Coding
21 Ways to make a Blended Family Work
I am
Marty learns to swim
30 days to being a better Christian
How to create an audio product
How to get Clients

Contents

Introduction

"Nobody makes it to the top without mentors and a powerful Master Mind team." Robert G. Allen

How to get clients requires several things to happen:

1) Taking responsibility for things the way they are. We can no longer put the blame on anyone else. The truth is if you really wanted more clients you would have them. A mind shift has to happen. What you have to do is realize you deserve it.
2) Believe in yourself.
3) Believe there is nothing wrong with achieving the level of success you deserve. Getting clients will require you do what you say you will do when you say you will do it. Massive Action is required, without it you will not get all of the clients you should be getting.

In the book E-Myth, Michael Gerber says "If they don't fail outright, most businesses fail to fully achieve their potential. That's because the person who owns the business doesn't truly know how to build a company that works without him or her...which is the key."

"Success is nothing more... than a few simple disciplines, practiced every day." Jim Rohn, author, motivational speaker, and business philosopher

According to Jay Lipe, "The first three times you promote something; you're really just creating awareness. The next twelve times you're reinforcing the awareness and beginning to uncover a need. And only by the twentieth time, will your prospect take action."

Pick which Marketing strategies you choose. The main thing to remember is you should spend two hours a day five days a week marketing or one full day during the week marketing. The more you promote the more you will sell and the more you will make assuming you have a good product or service.

Chapter 1 First things first

Decide what areas need improvement.

Where do you stand? What are your sales? What is your ROI? How many customers do you currently have?

Focus efforts. Stick to a Plan. Learn more. Determine goals for your business.

What actions will you take to accomplish them?

Develop customer focused strategies.

Develop Marketing

In order to increase your sales, it's time to focus on Income Producing Activities. What are you doing all day? How much time are you wasting? Think you don't waste time, think again. At the end of each day, ask yourself and be honest, did I focus on Income Producing Activities all day or Is what I did today moving me closer or farther away from meeting my goals. Using the 820/20 rule here as well, 20% of your activities/time will account for 80% of your sales. Pay attention to where time goes. Always work from a list. Do the most important things first.

What are you focused on? I know you are saying that you are busy but what are you busy doing? Will you focus on what actually brings you revenue?

"No matter what your product is, you are ultimately in the education business. Your customers need to be constantly educated about the many advantages of doing business with you, trained to use your products more effectively, and taught how to make never-ending improvement in their lives." Robert G. Allen Author of Multiple Streams of Income

This may seem simple, but you need to give customers what they want, not what you think they want. And, if you do this, people will keep coming back." Jack Ilhan, Australian businessman

"People react to buying messages for one of two reasons—to get pleasure or to avoid pain." (*Celebrity brand you*)

Jim Rohn said "Don't start the day until you have it finished. Don't start the week until you have it finished. Don't start the month until you have it finished. Plan your day."

What Jim Rohn meant by this is always plan your day before it starts, plan your week before it starts. Plan your month before it starts. This is so important. As entrepreneurs sometimes we can get caught up doing busy work but not the most important things we should be doing.

Always ask your customers how they heard about you. Use this form or make your own. You want to track where the clients you are getting are coming from.

I included these at the beginning for those who want to get started now. Also for those who won't finish this book.

101 Marketing Strategies

1. Determine how are you different (most important)
2. Networking
3. Brochures
4. Develop a Signature line to use for outgoing emails, forums, blog comments
5. Letterhead
6. Flyer
7. Door hangers
8. Tradeshow
9. Teach a class
10. Solo advertising
11. Newsletter
12. Sponsor an event
13. Catalogs
14. Bulletin Boards
15. Poster
16. Business Cards
17. Blog Writing/Posting
18. Blog Commenting
19. Forum Posts
20. Directory Submissions
21. http://www.bestbusinessdirectory.net/
22. DMOZ.org
23. www.business.com
24. www.allbusiness.com
25. www.yellowpapers.com
26. Facebook Ads
27. Linked in Ads
28. Tradeshows
29. Speaking Engagements
30. Yahoo Answers
31. Article Writing

32. Ezinearticles.com
33. Dimeco.com
34. Ideamarketer.com
35. Sooperaarticles.com
36. Buzzle.com
37. Isnare.com
38. Goarticls.com
39. Articlecity.com
40. Artcicletrader.com
41. Articlealley.com
42. Articlebase.com
43. Website Content Revision
44. Facebook
45. YouTube
46. Viddler
47. Vimeo
48. Metacafe
49. Daily Motion
50. Veoh
51. TubeMogul
52. Flickr
53. Twitter
54. Linked In
55. Link Exchange Campaign
56. PPC-Google, Yahoo
57. Google Places Local
58. Create Teleseminars
59. Create Webinars
60. Podcast
61. Demonstrations
62. Seminars
63. Write a White Paper
64. Product Launch
65. Sales Letters
66. Television

67. Radio
68. Newspaper
69. Press Releases
70. Search Engine Optimization
71. The title tag and page header are the two most important spots to put keywords
72. Research Keywords
73. Update content on site regularly
74. Create Site map
75. Write something for Digg
76. Create Squidoo Lens
77. Write something for Wikipedia
78. Write something for StumpleUpon
79. Delicious
80. Multiply
81. Reddit
82. Google Analytics
83. Create Hub pages
84. Sell e-books on Click bank
85. Sell products on eBay if applicable
86. Products/Services Blog Post Review
87. Get 25 likes/fans on Facebook so you can get your own URL
88. Include in your signature website address, Facebook, twitter and phone number
89. Pure 10 web 2.0
90. Link Wheel
91. Email marketing
92. Set up Auto responder with free e-course, newsletters
93. Run a contest
94. Use Alexa or Google toolbar to keep up PageRank
95. Check referrer log to see where visitors are coming from (PC World)
96. Use relevant words as anchor text within your website
97. For images, "Start with your image names: adding an "ALT" tag allows you to include a keyword-rich description for every

image on your site. The visible text around your images is valuable for SEO: Market Position suggests adding captions to all your pictures and being descriptive with the text in immediate physical proximity to your images.

98.   Hire a PR firm
99.   Hire a Copyrighter to assist with writing ads, sales letter etc.,
100.   Hire a Business Coach
101.   Set up RSS feed
102.   Podcast
103.   Affiliate Marketing
104.   Membership site
105.   Host your own Web Ring
106.   Become an expert on your local radio and television stations. Contact them for more information.
107.   Write a letter to the editor of local newspaper on a topic that you are an expert on
108.   Put a opt-in form on your website
109.   Strategic Alliances
110.   Write a booklet of tips
111.   Develop a PR kit
112.   Postcards
113.   Write a book
114.   Write an eBook
115.   Develop a home study course
116.   Develop an audio program
117.   Develop referral strategy
118.   Improve Sales Process
119.   Document frequent complaints (Consider changing process)
120.   Frequent Questions received should be added to FAQ (Frequently Asked Questions) section on your website
121.   Put documents on Google docs
122.   Put presentations on Slide share
123.   Packaging
124.   Presentations
125.   Signage

126. Develop strong call to action
127. Submit articles to e-zines
128. Submit articles to magazines
129. Speak at conferences
130. Join Professional Associations related to your target market
131. Join Board of Directors in your community
132. Volunteer in the community
133. Gather video testimonials (Put them on your website)
134. Use videos on your website (informational in nature)
135. Develop a system to turn customers into advocates
136. Develop an ideal client profile

Whether you are a small business owner or a sales professional there are key things you must do in order to increase sales.

1. Market like you never have before. Be sure you have segmented your market. Be sure you are targeting the right market with the right message at the right time. Create an Ideal Client Profile.
2. Up Sell and Cross sell every purchase. Write down all your products and services. Group those that are complimentary together.
3. Increase Prices 10%. Most businesses are charging less money than they should. If you charge what you are worth than you can deliver superior results.

"Accurately pricing your product is critical at any point in the economic cycle but no more so than in a recession," says Laura Willett, a small business consultant and faculty member in the finance department at Bentley College in Waltham, Mass

Chapter 2 Pricing

According to Ram Charan, "Profitable growth is everyone's business."

"Does your pricing structure reflect the value you provide customers? Does it also simultaneously improve revenue growth and the bottom line through effectively segmenting the customer's buying behavior and identifying the attributes the customer most values?"

What pricing strategy should you create for your products and services?

Do you price for profits and growth?

Do you just make up a price? Such as we charge 2 ½ times what the product cost to make?

Are your prices competitive?

1st Rule is Pricing Don't start low and expect to raise prices later.

2nd Pricing has a lot to do with perception. How are you perceived in the marketplace?

3rd Rule of Pricing Add value that means something to the customer.

As Jayashree Pakhave said in a recent article "Only 20% of your customers buy on price, so why bother with these customers." They tend to cause more problems and tend to want more and more for less and less.

In *How to price your product* Paul F. Roberts writes "Business owners in competitive markets also need to find a way to distinguish the goods and services they offer from those of other, larger competitors, Wikelt and Fenno agree.

"When you look at pricing, it's not just a multiple of your cost. Its what customers are willing to pay and the perceived quality of the goods. Customers will usually be willing to pay more if you have a better product than someone else," Willett said Paul F. Roberts.

There are many ways to price a product.

"You must charge a premium price so you have a large margin to provide an extraordinary value and experience."

In *Keeping Score*, Mark Graham Brown said "People's perception of value is based on their knowledge of the cost of similar items, and what they are willing to pay for quality, prestige, rarity and other factors that determine the price of goods and services in the marketplace. Customer satisfaction is an important determinant of future buying behavior, but not nearly as important as customers' perception of value for their dollars."

Tips on Pricing

Pricing should be realistic and fair.

Sell on value

Assess your prices on a regular basis to ensure you are maximizing profits

Know what your competitors charge

Twelve things to consider when Pricing your products and services

What is the perception of the customer? Are your products and services identical to the competition?

What is your competition charging? Is it comparable to what you are offering?

What are customers expecting to pay?

How much does it cost you to perform or develop your product or service?

What value can you offer?

What is your profit margin? What is your current ROI? How many of that product or service do you sell?

Who is in the top 20% of your customers? Where does the top 20% of your customer come from?

Why should a prospective customer buy from you?

What promises do you make with your product or service?

What profit do you want to make on your product or service?

How do I want to be perceived in the market?

What are you trying to accomplish with your pricing?

Most small business owners struggle to determine the right price for their product or service. Price is a very important part of the Marketing Mix. In my experience most prices are too low. If we price our products or services incorrectly we could be losing money either because our price is too low or because it's too high. How do you currently come up with your prices?

It is vital to know what your competition is charging. 90% of business owners don't know. Most people feel they are too busy and that guessing is best. Not only is knowing the prices your competitors charge important but also what is included in that price. Where are they weak? Where can you add value that would prove to be important to the client?

Pricing your product or service at the right price can be tricky. The wrong price will either cause you too loose money or lose customers. When choosing your pricing strategy, always keep in mind what pricing structure is used by your industry (this can be determined by industry association website). What is the cost for you to produce the product or service? Pricing has to be consistent with the position you want to take in the market. Take into consideration the customer's perception of your price.

Know what your competitors charge. Get a friend to pretend to be a customer. Check competitor's websites for prices. Are your prices competitive? Are your prices higher or lower than your competition?

Test different prices and see which one responds to better.

Consider the Lifetime Value of your customer. Is it necessary to lose money on the first sale to obtain that customer in the long term and make money on that customer for years to come?

Research indicates that a 1 percent increase in price boosts profits two or three times as much as a 1 percent increase in sales volume.

A Study by McKinsey and Company of the Global 1200 found that if they increased their prices by just 1%, and demand remained constant, on average each company's operating profits would increase by 11%.

Choosing the right price is important to business success. If your prices are too high, you risk only getting a few sales. If your prices are too low, you might be bombarded with sales but you leave a lot of money on table thus less revenue for your company. Choosing the right price becomes more and more important as customers demand more and more for less and less. Customers have to be educated on the value of your product or service. Explain to customers the dangers, mistakes, revenue loss, or increase in cost they will experience when they don't do business with you.

Choosing a low price will often make you dread doing the work when the time comes. This shouldn't be the deciding factor but only one part of the equation. All costs should be considered when deciding the price. Also check with associations in your industry for pricing information such as do most business in your industry charge a retainer, hourly rate, per project, etc.

"Prices should be high enough so that the business makes a profit and yet low enough to keep customers coming through the door."

Pricing Strategy

1. Research association and industry practices. Research competition to see what they are charging
2. Test different prices
3. Determine what it cost to produce the product or service. What is the Labor/equipment/supplies? What are your fixed costs? How can you add value?
4. Determine Pricing Approach
5. Review current pricing structure. What are the margins of each product or service?
6. Use multiple methods to calculate your price

Why most small businesses price products or services too low?

- Miscalculating costs
- Inadequate market research
- Ignorance-Not knowing any other way
- Desperate to make sales-thinking that they can raise prices later

Small business owners price the product or service haphazardly not really taking into consideration the loss of revenue. Pricing is one of the most important decisions a business owner is faced with.

Action Steps

Review your Pricing of every product or service

Determine how much profit you will make on each product or service

Set up a Pricing strategy for each product or service

Review Competitors Sites for Pricing Info

Determine how products are different. Similar

Review Industry Sites. What is the Standard Pricing Strategy? Hourly? Per Project?

What is the Average?

What is it for your area?

Evaluate whether you can provide your product or service cheaper, better and quicker.

How to figure out your pricing

Figure out what your fixed costs are.

Figure out what your variable costs are.

Figure out the costs to manufacture or create services.

Figure out the amount you want to be paid hourly, per month, yearly.

Figure out how much you want to make per hour based on yearly rate.

You should make enough to pay all your fixed and variable costs plus pay yourself a salary and have money left to leave in your business.

How to increase sales

1) Study other industries to see what they are doing. Try a few things other industries use as best practices.
2) Talk to everyone everywhere you go. Don't be bashful. Strike up a conversation and start talking.
3) Focus Focus Focus on one thing until it is done. As Entrepreneurs we can easily start 100 things but finish none of them.
4) Develop a Plan. "If you are failing to plan, you are failing to plan." A plan is essential for growth. Start with a list of things you need to do to increase your sales. Add to it as you come across more things that need to be done. "Create a definite plan for carrying out your desire, and begin at once, whether you're ready or not, to put it into action." -- Napoleon Hill
5) Know where you are now. First things first what is your current sales volume now. What is the total number of sales currently? Also determine what is the total by product or service. Use the 80/20 Rule here what are your top 20% of the products or services

6) Determine where you want to be. What are your sales goals? If you are a business owner you will also want to write down your profitability goals? You can break these down by month, week or even day. This will give you a gauge on which to work on daily. Before you begin a thing, remind yourself that difficulties and delays quite impossible to foresee are ahead... You can only see one thing clearly, and that is your goal. Form a mental vision of that and cling to it through thick and thin" says Kathleen Norris. What are the goals of the business? Are you on target to reach those goals? Do you have goals in place for your business? Sales, Profitability, leads, conversations

Research indicates if you do what they do long enough, you will see the results they get.

"20% of what we do leads to 80% of the results."-Richard Koch

As business planning expert Time Berry knows, "You must expect growth by planning for it."

Are you targeting the right target market? Do you have customers that you need to fire because they drain all your energy? Develop an ideal client profile. Start to weed out customers or clients who don't fit your ideal client profile.

When was the last time you asked for referrals? Start sending a referral letter at least every 3 months to past clients or business associates (those in your network). Make sure you give referrals as well. Develop a referral strategy. Don't be ashamed to ask for them.

Develop a roadmap. There are probably at least 10 things you've been meaning to do to grow your business and just haven't. Well now is the time. Write them down, along with everything else you have to do to accomplish your goals. Don't limit yourself. You can accomplish twice as much as you are currently by prioritizing and doing what is important and delegating the rest.

Take the most important Goal and write it down. Create a plan to achieve it.

What strategies you will use to accomplish them?

Offer a range of products or services if you don't already. Upsell, crossell or downsell every sale. Show prospects the value you offer. Offer complimentary products and services together. Listen to your customers, they will tell you what they need and where their pain and pleasure points are.

Activate old customers. Do you have a system in place to activate old customers? If not, it's time to get one. Research indicates that it cost 5 to 6 times as much to acquire a new one then to retain an old one.

What are 10 ways you can activate old customers?

1. Email/autoresponder
2. Coupons
3. Card (Holiday, Thank You for your business)
4. Send a Notepad every few months
5. Ask customers to complete a Survey (How can we best serve you?)
6. Email your customers relevant articles

7. Through Social Media

Customer Loyalty Strategy

A loyalty strategy will help you grow your business by attracting and retaining the right customers as well as employees. A loyalty strategy also helps to track the behavior of customers and employees. Do you know who your top buyers are? If not, you need to find out right away where the top 80% of your business comes from. This will represent 20% of your clients and customers. This is vital to your staying in business.

Customer Retention

Do you know how much it cost to acquire a new customer? "According to Bain and Company, Over a 5 Year period a company may lose as many as ½ of their customers.

Acquiring a new customer can cost 6 to 7 times more than retaining an existing customer.

Chapter 3 Business Strategy

Business Strategy is one of your greatest assets in business. It provides your business if done right a competitive advantage.

What is a business strategy you might ask

A business strategy is a written plan. A strategy is a clear understanding of what it is you do and how you can help your target market. A strategy also addresses where you want to be in the future, but more importantly how you plan to get there. A business strategy requires some thought and careful planning.

What is your mission?

What are your business goals?

Who are your competitors (external environment)?

What are your business's strengths and weakness (internal environment)?

How will you Implement your strategy (tactics)?

How will you measure your performance? For example cost per units, units per employee per year.

Jay Abraham author of The Sticking Point Solution says "Change your strategy, change your results."

Kelley Summer 2009 GM 105 Strategic Management says "A strategy is a business approach to a set of competitive moves that are designed to generate a successful outcome" "A strategy is management's game plan for

- o Strengthening the organization's competitive position

- o Satisfying customers
- o Achieving performance targets

Dr. Pete Johnson says "A successful strategy-be it marketing, sales, or business-tends to follow several key principles.

Principle #1 A strategy should be simple. The more complicated we make it the more difficult it may be to implement or to adapt to our ever changing market environment.

Principle #2 A strategy should be quick. It should not take an exhausting amount of time to develop, let alone execute.

Principle #3 A strategy should be capable of producing very immediate, visible, measurable results. The watch-words-here are. How soon, How much."

"According to C.K. Prahalad and Gary Hamel's ground breaking article ("The Core Competencies of the Corporation" Harvard Business review, May/June 1990), the key to a sound business strategy is to do something that others cannot do, or do something well that others do poorly, or have great difficulty doing well." (*Keeping Score*, Mark Graham Brown)

In How Successful People Think Bob Biehl, the author of *Masterplanning*

- o Direction: What should we do next? Why?
- o Organization: Who is responsible for what? Who is responsible for whom? Do we have the right people in the right places?
- o Cash: What is our projected income, expense, net? Ca we afford it? How can we afford it?
- o Tracking: Are we on target?

- Overall Evaluation: Are we achieving the quality we expect and demand of ourselves?
- Refinement: How can we be more effective and more efficient (move toward the ideal)?

Creating a Strategic Plan

Strategic Planning is critical to the longevity or life of your business. If you don't have one, chances are you are on the way out of business. Strategic Planning is vital to big and small businesses. Small businesses often overlook this important step but it provides numerous benefits.

Strategic Planning helps small business owners get focused, set goals and plan for challenges and growth. Planning allows an organization to put things into an orderly and systematic way.

"The Process by which the leaders of an organization determine what the organization wants to look like at the end of a specified period of time-usually three to five years-then use that vision to establish multiyear goals and objectives which describe what the organization wishes to accomplish and develop programs, tasks, and timelines for achieving them. Long-range planning predicts future conditions and realities, internal and external, and plans how the organization can function effectively within them."

"To achieve great things, two things are needed A plan and not quite enough time." Leonard Bernstein

A Good Business destined for success starts with a plan. Without it that business is destined for failure. Entrepreneurs and Small Businesses alike hate planning. It is the key to your success.

Most entrepreneurs are quick to say they have a plan but when I ask to look over it they tell me it is in their head. But a true plan needs to be written down on paper. Something happens when you write down your plan first things become more real and second issues or problems that you haven't considered will surface. Take the time to write down your plan, it will save you time and money in the long run. Plans provide direction and focus. You don't have to guess because you have a blueprint from which to follow. It doesn't have to be perfect. Nor does it mean it can't be changed because it can be as needed. Also you might be saying "I don't know all the steps necessary," it is important to do some research and model your plan after someone who has achieved the success you desire. There is plenty of information out there.

"Having an effective growth planning system is the best indicator of whether your company will grow." Steven S Little, Author

"A single sheet of paper is enough to describe your organization vision, mission, values, objectives and strategies, plus help focus on individual priorities." Joe Calhoon

"Effective Planning Strengthens people, productivity, and profitability. Joe Calhoon

Plans you should have

Business Plan

Marketing Plan

Strategic Plan

Internet Marketing Plan

Social Media Plan

3 P's of Planning

Preparation

Persistence

Passion

Specific

Strategic Planning

Where am I to date? Cash flow?

Where are you getting those results?

Where do I want to be?

How will I get there?

Mission/Vision

Where are you now? 2 customers a day

Where do you want to be? Goals

What are you currently doing? Making 1 Sales call a month. Double that. Then Double that and so on.

What can you do each day to improve your situation?

What is your plan/road map for improving your position? Think long term

Measure everything

Market everywhere

Make someone's day

Mimic success around you

Chapter 4 Business Growth

Business Growth is built on a foundation. It is structured. It rarely happens on accident. Business Growth is systematic in nature. It requires steps to work together for the ultimate goal of growth (business)

Business Growth requires a strategy

The key to Strategy Development

Where are we?

Where do we want to go

How will we get there?

How much will it cost?

What will have to be done daily?

Sample Small Business Strategy

For example, increase sales by 20%.

Hire a PR Firm.

Implement Social Media Campaign

Optimize your website

Document leads where they are coming from

Document Conversion rate

Test landing page

Work on Sales Process

Listen to Customers

Keep it simple

Take 1 step at time

Be flexible

Change as necessary

Create a timeline

Budget Accordingly

Chapter 5 Metrics

Do you have metrics in place to determine whether or not your business is making progress?

Jack Welch, former chairman and CEO, General Electric says "Too often we measure everything and understand nothing. The three most important things you need to measure in a business are customer satisfaction, employee satisfaction, and cash flow."

According to Micheal LeBoeuf, PhD, Author and Consultant indicates that "Picking the right numbers to track for your business is one of the most important decisions you can make. People do what gets measured."

"Research funded by Harvard Business School found that companies that: obsessively" focused on meeting customers; employees', and owners' need-While developing readership at all levels-outperformed comparison companies in four critical areas:

1. Revenues increase 4 times faster.
2. Job creation is 7 times greater.
3. Owner equity grows 12 times faster.
4. Profit performance is 756 times higher.

The first thing you have to do is to accept the realization that if you don't do anything, then nothing is going change. Things will continue to spiral out of control. If you are reading this, chances are you want to make the effort to turn this business around. It is important to determine what your goals are.

What everyone should know about their business?

1) Performance metrics

What if you make subtle changes in your Marketing?

ROI

# of sales

Average sales (Dollar Amount)

# of leads

Conversion Rates

2) Customer loyalty/advocates

Top 20% customers

Bottom 20% customers

Who are your most profitable customers? How often they buy?

Who are your least profitable customers? Fire them.

3) Target market

in market

Business/consumer

Revenue/amount of money you need to make

Buying patterns

4) Competitors

Who are your competitors?

What are their Strengths?

How are you different? What can you improve upon? Your weakness

5) Cash flow now How much cash do you have right now? Make sure it is current and as accurate as possible. It may be less than you think. At the current where will you be in 3 months? 6 months?

Test and Track the changes

How did you hear about us?

How do you measure up to your competitors?

Metrics are essential to every small business owner. Business owners especially small business owners cannot afford to waste money on Marketing or anything else that is not working. "What gets measured gets managed."

Metrics provide answers into whether we are making progress toward our strategic goals.

Sample Metrics

Sales Metrics
- ✓ Average customer size
- ✓ % of repeat business
- ✓ Cost to gain new customers
- ✓ Customer profitability
- ✓ Average sales per customer per year

HR metrics
- ✓ Job satisfaction score of employees measured by surveys
- ✓ Employee retention
- ✓ Employee attrition
- ✓ Turnover rate due to poor performance
- ✓ Turnover rate for the year without notice

Business metrics
- ✓ Cash on hand
- ✓ Total value of overdue invoices

Chapter 6 Marketing

Make sure marketing is relevant and meaningful to your target market. The purpose of it is to get them to visit your website or call you on the phone.

Marketing Tactics

1. Blog daily. Stay in touch with customers. Offer your advice. Make a list and add to it whenever you get an idea. Use this list to write articles on your blog. Visit forums to get ideas for new topics or answer questions found in forums in your blog giving credit to that person, of course.
2. Write articles weekly. Submit to the top 10 article directories. This is a great way to get maximum exposure. If you don't have time, outsource it to Upwork, fiverr or Guru.com. Make sure articles have good content and reflect your expertise in the services or products you offer.
3. PR. Send out Press Releases when you have a new product or service. Use PR leads and Expert Click for maximum exposure. Outsource the writing of the Press Release if you need too.
4. Answer questions on LinkedIn and Facebook. Make sure you use your signature with your name, website, email (if allowed) and Company name.
5. Set up Social alerts relevant to your specialization. Comment on these websites/forum/blogs that are relevant to your niche.
6. Set up RSS feeds to be the first to comment on high traffic sites. How many leads are you receiving? How many sales? Work to increase that number.
7. Use an autoresponder and make it automatic. Stay in touch with your customers. Build your list by offering a free 5 day ecourse.

8. Crossell and Upsell to clients. Offer complimentary products or services on each purchase or the next highest product or service in the category or group. No, they won't buy every time usually about 30% of the time but 30% adds up fast.
9. Offer a free teleseminar/demonstration. Educate your customers on your product or service. I like Chet Holmes suggestion, You can do something like a Core story or a 5 deadly mistakes related to your topic.

Marketing Process

The Marketing Process can be a hard, long one. Marketing has to be done at the right time to the right people.

The Marketing Process is basically a system which is built on a solid foundation which is your target market. The Marketing Process must include a budget and a timeframe from which Marketing is taking place.

The Marketing Process requires knowledge of your target market. The more you know the better. Creating an ideal client profile will answer key questions to better assist your customers. It will also allow you when the time comes to drop the bottom 20% of your customers.

Having a process is no good without solid metrics in place. It is necessary to know what is working and what is not. It is also good to know how many prospects you are getting from your marketing vs. how many are being converted to sales. Knowing this will only help you improve this number and ultimately add more to the bottom line.

Testing one thing at a time in your ad or website page to see if results improve or not. You will be surprised at how a change in color or font size can increase sales.

The Marketing Process requires numerous touchpoints. According to Research, your potential prospect has to see your message or advertisement 7 to 9 times before they even notice you, which means it will probably take even more exposures to get them to buy.

While Social Media and technology is taking a majority of advertising dollars today, offline is not dead yet. A mixture of Online and Offline Marketing is still necessary for every business marketing strategy.

Marketing Success

Marketing Success takes hard work and time. But with careful attention your marketing will be a success and so will your Business.

How will you reach them? Will you have to engage them on Facebook?

Create an Ideal Client Profile. Who is your target market?

Create Marketing Message. What is your message? Are you educating your clients? Are you benefits clear? What is appealing?

Create Metrics (Marketing). It is important to determine ROI on each Marketing Campaign, # of leads, # of presentations, # of sales.

Create a Marketing Campaign. What channels will you use to reach your market? How long will this campaign last?

Create a Timeline. Is it 3 months, 4 months or 6 months?

Touch points. How many touch points will take place during this campaign with this customer? Will there be 3, 5, 7 or 10 touch points?

Determine the budget. How much money can you spend consistently? Monthly or Quarterly? What will that money be used for? Consistency is key.

Create a Unique Selling Proposition (USP). Why should someone buy from you and not your competitors? What makes you better?

Create a Strong call 2 action. What do you want your target market to do in response to your Marketing? Can they tell in a few seconds your message and what they need to do next?

You want to determine who your top 5 competitors are. Constantly raise the bar. Strive to be better and do better. This is important as somewhat of a gauge of industry standards. Determine how you are better. How are they better? Without taking time to conduct research and careful analysis you will never know.

Determine what customers really want. Do you know? Customer's needs are changing so quickly. Don't be caught not knowing.

Segment market. Every business can break their target market into smaller pieces. The key is focusing on the most profitable piece which is not always the biggest piece.

Develop a follow up process. What will you do to stay in contact with your customers? Will you use a newsletter? Develop a conversion strategy. How will you convert each prospect into a sale? Determine what it will take now and work that plan.

How to get the most from your Marketing?

If you have a business, you need to have a Marketing Plan as well as a budget in place. If not figure out how much you can afford to put towards your marketing. This is one of the most important elements in your business. Because no Marketing=No business.

If you are just starting out this number will probably be higher. The recommended average is 1 to 2% of what you expect your annual salary is. Marketing is an investment in your business future not an expense. But it has to be done right.

When was the last time you asked a client or customer, how did you hear about us? If you are not doing it, start now. Also include it on online purchases as well.

There is no sense throwing money out the window (or wasting money on Marketing that is not working). Of course sometimes it just needs a little tweaking. If you have a website (and in this day and age, I hope you do) you should be growing your list. Offer prospects something of value (Lead Magnet) in exchange for their name and email address. Use an autoresponder program like Aweber, Infusion Soft or Constant Contact to stay in contact with your prospects.

You've spent the time getting them there you may as well get them into your funnel and build a relationship with you by staying in contact with them daily, weekly or biweekly. This will allow you to sell them after they learn more about you and your products and services.

Positioning

Positioning is how consumers perceive your product or service in relation to your competitors. "What is the position of the product in the mind of the consumer?" Trout and Ries suggest a six-step question framework for successful positioning:

1. What position do you currently own?
2. What position do you want to own?
3. Whom you have to defeat to own the position you want?
4. Do you have the resources to do it?

5. Can you persist until you get there?
6. Are your tactics supporting the positioning objective you set?

Positioning is about perception. What you value might not be the same as what your customer value? Quality might be important to me and money to you. Positioning only occurs after segmentation of the market has taken place.

This framework is a great start to improve your positioning in the marketplace. Positioning is a work in progress and not a destination.

10 Marketing Questions to ask yourself

1. Do my customers know what to do after seeing my Marketing piece (strong call to action)?
2. Will potential customers see my message 7 or more times?
3. Do I have a set goal or goals for each campaign?
4. Do I have a budget for each campaign?
5. Is my message consistent?
6. Am I spending at least 8 hours Marketing per week?
7. Am I asking every person who makes a purchase, how did they hear about us?
8. Do I have metrics in place to determine the success of the campaign?
9. Do I have all my eggs in one basket?
10.   Could I use the help of an expert on this campaign (mailing services, graphic designer, copywriter)?

Writing a Marketing Plan

Writing a Marketing Plan can prove to be tedious. But it is very important to your small business growth. Businesses cannot grow to their full potential without a marketing plan. A marketing plan often shows up weaknesses and threats or business problems that you had not previously considered.

The first thing is determining your target market. Do you really know who your target market is? Where they work, education, age, income level, etc.

For businesses do you know the size of the company, sales/profits/publications they read.

What problems does your product solve? How does your product do that?

In *Leap! 101 Ways to Grow Your Business*, Stephanie Chandler wrote "If you aren't generating leads steadily, it's time to get aggressive and test new strategies until you come up with a process that you can take to the bank."

Peter Drucker, management guru says, "Business has only two basic functions: marketing and innovation. Marketing and innovation produce results. All the rest are costs."

Action Items

Know Your Business

Industry

Target Market

Competitors

# of contacts before someone notices you

Develop a Marketing Plan

Set Goals. Write them down.

"Segmented market produce the greatest sales potential." "Focus on the most targeted segments of the market, the one you can serve best."

Determine Budget for year and then determine what you can do monthly to develop a campaign. Without a plan, your efforts will be scattered and your results not measureable. Marketing consistency wins customers long before you need them. "Remember that the only thing you'll get from less marketing is less business." "Today, small targeted, relentless marketing is often the difference between a business that has reached a plateau and one that has reached its potential."

Marketing should be done all year long. Marketing should be done whether business is good or bad. Marketing should be done in a recession more and with precision. Marketing should be measured and analyzed at least monthly. Marketing should be done as if in the customer's shoes. What gets your attention? Marketing goals is a necessity. How do you know if your marketing was successful or not without goals?

Marketing Campaign

For this example, I will use 3 months, Marketing should be done over a variety of outlets (online, offline, advertising, social media and mediums) (Google Adwords, Facebook, direct mail)

3 month campaigns are great.

   1. Determine the length of the campaign.

2. Determine how much you can invest in marketing activities. Be careful with this as it should be representative of projected or actual sales. If you spend the bare minimum this is likely what you will get in return.
3. Determine the variety of outlets you will use to Market your products and services. An ideal client profile will help you determine where this should be based on where the target market spends their time.
4. Determine Marketing Goals.
5. Determine Metrics used for this campaign to measure its effectiveness.
6. Start Marketing.
7. Test to see what is working and what is not. Make subtle changes to see if results improve. Continue to adjust as needed.
8. After measuring ROI, do more of what works and stop doing what isn't.

"A good set of metrics will allow me to predict that if I spend $1 on a certain marketing tactic, I'm likely to get $X of revenue in Y days. A good set of metrics will also give you a feel for inside or outside sales effectiveness and overall sales pipeline velocity as well." (Marketing Metrics 101 for B2B Startups)

USPs (Unique Selling Proposition) must be done with the customer in mind. USPs should be important to the customer- something they want. USPs should be one that the competition cannot, or does not offer.

"Marketing is the bedrock of virtually every enduring dominate business in every field. You must be a superior marketer. The good news is that great marketers are made, not born. Learning how to market efficiently, powerfully, and profitably is a simple and surprisingly logical process" says Jay Abraham.

Identify what your business is doing now in each of these categories.

Is the approach I'm using to generate and sustain business anywhere close to the highest and best approach out there?

Creation of an integrated, detailed growth plan, for the year.

Broken down backward by product by market by marketing, by source, by type of buyer, by month, and sometimes even by week.

Test and adjust.

If it's down, you'll adjust by replacing activities fine tuning your approach, or adding new lines of attack.

You must be passionate for what you're doing and for whom you're doing it.

Are you focusing on the wrong things?

Test one new approach to selling, marketing, or advertising and then test a second approach and then a third approach. One might prove to be better than another.

Marketing message has to be all about the customer not you.

How will they find out about your products or services?

How much are they willing to pay for your products or services?

How are you different from your competitors? Better? Worst?

Who are your competitors?

Research 5 to 10 of your competitors.

Marketing Metrics

New Inquires

Source of Leads

New Customer Sales

New Product Revenue

Profitability by project or customer

Cost per Inquiry (CPI)

Cost per order

The single most important question to ask every customer.

How did you hear about us?

Measure your marketing efforts

Analyze lead generation efforts at least monthly

How many leads are you receiving monthly

Where are they coming from?

How many of those leads are you closing?

How can this # be improved? Pitfalls

Evaluate closing process

Get focused. Is your message focused on 1 or 2 benefits that your customers care about?

Action Items

Develop your own White Paper.

Continually fill your prospect pipeline

Make sure it is clear what your product or service does.

Does your target market know how to get your product or service and how to use it properly?

Write a direct mail letter

Ask for referrals

Implement a referral strategy

Consider hiring outside help when needed whether it be a copywriter or graphic designer

Be patient and persistent

Use consistent imagery and messages throughout your marketing

What does your marketing say about your company? Is it cheesy? Is it well thought out?

According to John Jantsch in Marketing Strategy, "Consider firing about 20 percent of your past customers simply on the basis that they no longer fit into the picture of your current business"

Start with your target market

Then choose your positioning

Establish your brand

This will guide your advertising, promotion and pricing

Focus Focus Focus on your target customers

Execute your strategy well

Coordinate, concentrate and communicate efforts

1. Target market
2. Business Objectives: revenue, profits, cash flow, units sold, market share
3. Positioning one or two key benefits
4. Programs (tactics or marketing mix) (pricing advertising, personal selling, distribution)

"20 percent of my advertising brings in 80 percent of my business, but I don't know which 20 percent!" This is the mistake that most small business owners make they don't know which part of your advertising is working.

Over 12 months what would you do to gain exposure for your business

Action Items

List Competitors

List Prices/Costs

List Vulnerabilities

List Unique Selling Proposition

Strengths

Weakness

Competitive Advantage

Ask customers what in your product or service do they value

Marketing Campaign

List months   Budget   /Types of Marketing

Commit 1 hour to 2 hours a day

Test and measure everything

Ideal Client Profile

Business-to-Consumer

Age_____

Gender_____

Geographic
Location_____

Type of
users_____

Household
income_____

Behavior_____

Marital
Status_____

Family
Structure_____

Education_____

Children/No Children_____

Home owner or Rental_____

Ideal Client Profile

Business-to-Business

Location

_____

Number of Employees

_____

Years in business _____

Specialty or Type of business

_____

Size of Company

_____

Revenue

_____

Number of Departments

_____

Industry

_____

Public or Private

Other_____

Chapter 7 Systems

"Your business life is a machine with a variety of moving parts. If any of these parts are defective, the entire machine can come to a grinding stop."-- Brian Tracy

Are you feeling overwhelmed and not getting everything you need done?

Are you working 60+hours a week?

Are you trying to do repetitive tasks?

If you answered yes to any of these questions, then it's time to create systems in your business. Are you serious about growing your business, then creating systems is a must.

Systems allow your business to run without you. Systems are one of the building blocks of business growth. Systems are created on activities that are done on a repetitive basis.

Creating systems gains clarity and focus.

Creating systems puts the business owner in control. It takes the business owner from working in the business to working on the business.

Creating systems creates a turnkey business that runs without you.

"Success is not inherent in the act of franchising the business, but rather in the formula owners use in organizing and operating the business as a turnkey system. And the power of this franchise formula can be applied to any business anytime, anywhere to achieve maximum productivity and profitability."

Bradley J Sugars raises an interesting question could you wake up in the morning and call your office and say to whoever answered you all hold the fort. I am taking of the next three months. "Would there be mass panic or would things run smoothly while you were gone. Would you be so worried about your business that you couldn't take three months off. Well if you would like to get into a position to take three months off and be free from worry listen to the following very closely.

"Management works in the system. Leadership works on the system." Stephen R. Covey

Susan Carter offers the following advice

"Write down the steps and procedures to accomplish each task associated with the job.

Make it a learnable procedure by using the words, "Step one, step two, etc."

Be as detailed as possible

For each action, ask yourself why you are doing it this way. Write it down.

Organizational Chart

Job Description

Start delegating routine tasks that can easily be done someone else. How much time are you wasting and therefore losing money that can be easily be done by someone else? As long as you continue to do minuscule tasks your business will never reach its full potential. Just think the next time you start doing some administrative tasks just look at it like flushing money down the drain or money going out the window. Who can afford to lose money in this economy. No one. So start delegating.

"If you continue to work in your business and not on it then your business will never grow and prosper. If you are going to keep working in your business and not on it then realize you've just bought yourself a job." Sugars

Systems take time to create. Systems are simple. Systems have to be tweaked and updated regularly. People work the systems. "A business system is a combined document of the company's different policies, procedures and processes. This document is used to train and guide new employees and to make the company run efficiently."

Training is required after these systems are in place. Use lists when creating systems. Simple Flow Charts work well. Use Visual aid such as pictures.

Do you have a favorite recipe that you like to cook? Have you ever found yourself, if you let a considerable amount of time lapse between cooking it if you don't glance back at the recipe you forget one of the steps or ingredients?

This is similar to a business, because we are all human. We sometimes forget and systems allow us consistency and also a framework (place to go back and look to make sure we don't forget anything. This is especially important for those tasks or activities that you do less frequently).

Systems provide a great way to train new staff.

Brian Tracy says "Your steps should be written by a genius so clearly that they can be followed by a moron."

A very important part of systems is they should be detailed so someone off the streets could take the steps or instructions and compile the task.

A system is a process.

Document every segment of your business as a system.

Systems are the foundation of every great company.

Start Working on your Business, not in your business.

It is vitally important to create systems in your business.

Have you created a job or a business?

If you need help running these systems consider hiring friends, family, some of your own subscribers, Marketing forums (Warrior Forum), Outsourcing to Guru, Upwork, Craiglist.

As a business owner you put the systems in place so it will work whether you are there or not. McDonalds is a great example of a franchise prototype to use. It doesn't matter if you go to a McDonalds in Japan or California everything is fixed the same way. There are procedures on everything they do (proven systems). Duplication in another location is possible because of the systems. It is amazing how well it runs.

If you ever want to sell your business, you have to have systems in place. Systems are well documented. Systems are organized. Make a list of all the systems you think you want to create. Write down what you do each day, each month, each week. Next you will have to figure out how you will document your procedures and what resources or tools are you going to use. Then break each of those activities down into individual steps. Make sure to write down step-by-step process. For example, writing a blog, writing an article.

Write it, Edit it and then demonstrate it on video. On computer, you can use Camtasia recording to do this on Camtasia. Free trial, (free program available CamStudio.org) is available. You can do it with a camcorder or photos. Create a template or checklist to ensure all steps are done and done correctly.

Michael E. Gerber in E Myth Mastery talks about creating job descriptions.

Sample systems

Here are a few that will jog your memory and give you an idea to get started.

Phone Systems Incoming

Phone Systems Outgoing

Sales Training Process (Training)

Marketing

Customer Resolution Process

Preparing a Quote

Follow up Systems

Conversion Strategy

Complete Sales Process

Handling Payments

Prospecting (Generating new clients)

Handling new customers

Hiring System

Accounts payable

Accounts receivable

How to processes into function groups

Business Management

Finance and Accounting

Sales and Marketing

Operations

Customer Service

Personnel

IT Computer Systems

Safety and Security

Opening Procedures

Closing Procedures

Return Procedures (Return Policy should be included)

Repair System (What steps are needed to repair something. Possibly a form completed)

Production System (List all steps from start to finish)

Pricing Systems

Subsystems in each

Administration

Research and Development

Accounting Systems

Billing

Distribution

Production (replenishing stock)

Lead Generation System

Shipping/receiving

Quality Control

Collections

Custodial

Website

Product development

Cash development

Information systems

Facilities Management

Communications

Standard Operating Procedures

Purchasing

Financial Management Systems

One of the keys to success in business is the development of systems. All great businesses have systems. Systems tell an employee

When to do something (monthly, weekly daily)

How to do something (step by step instructions on how some task is to be done)

Why/relevance of a task (purpose)

Who should do the task

Systems are multifaceted.

Systems provide an organized and efficient way of doing things in business. It takes the guess work out. It provides a framework which should be improved upon and updated regularly. It helps a business to run like a well-oiled machine.

Systems are great because they allow you to leverage your time. In other words, instead of you working 80 hours a week doing all of the work with a system you can hire other people to help you. It frees up your time to do other things that are more important. Quite often when a business owner works this many hours with minimal results there is a lot that can be delegated and focus on more critical issues that are being neglected. Systems are easy to create and a necessity for all businesses.

Systems that are detail oriented and accurate will produce better results.

Four steps to creating a system

Start with the department closest to the money. In other words, when money exchanges hands with client and yourself. From their work backwards

Provide examples

Get each staff member to write down what they do in detail daily, weekly, monthly

Without proper systems in place you are wasting valuable resources (time and money). All systems with a business combine to form an operations manual. Most businesses think they can't afford to put the manpower into developing and writing down the systems within a business. When the truth his you can't afford not to put those systems in place.

Question all systems

Why do we do it his way?

Is there a better way?

Why most business don't have systems in place to run their business?

1. Systems take too much time to develop.
2. They don't understand the value of systems.
3. They never heard of systems.
4. They are buried underneath so many other important jobs.

Each department or function should have a system. Just because you have a system for your accounts receivables doesn't mean you don't have to have a system for taking orders.

Don't' let short term opportunities deter you from achieving long term goals.

Document processes working directly with customers.

Always have the person currently performing task or process to write it down step by step. If you are working alone, choose task that are most cumbersome and time consuming. Ideally you want to delegate this to someone or outsource it after adequate training takes place.

Systems should be wrote down in the order they are to be completed.

Start with three business activities and then the next three activities until you have your systems and operations manual completed.

Consider your business a franchise prototype. If you were to create a franchise. You would have to have systems in place so everything is done the same way at every location. When people buy franchises they are buying proven systems that work, which is why the failure rate for franchises is so low. The purpose for doing this to create a blueprint for your specific business that can be replicated anywhere in the world. Sounds easy enough. Let's get started.

Initially systems require some work and extra effort and even a little expense to set up but once it is set up you have a turnkey business that will run without you. This will free up your time to do tasks that will grow your business and you can hire someone to work the systems. Make sense. Systems allow you to work on the business instead of in the business.

Why should you create systems?

Benefits of systems

Predictable and Measurable results
Increase Productivity
Makes things easier and simpler
Frees your time up
Increase Profits
Builds consistency and reliability
Increases efficient
Increases your chances of selling business
Reduces Mistakes
Business Runs smoothly
Improves Operations
Yields Extraordinary results

Promotes Continuous learning, growth and improvement of individuals and organizations
Customers get what they want every time
Provide quality
Accomplish objectives
Achieve maximum customer loyalty, profitability and growth

Systems are the solution to
Poor performance
Wasted Resources
Customer Dissatisfaction
Employee Turnover
Excessive Costs
Weak Sales Growth
Poor cash flow
Low Profit
Daily frustrations
Every business Roadblock

After completing Systems must continually ask yourself

How can we do this better, cheaper, faster?

"A systems-dependent business = Repeatable performance = consistent results = A business that virtually runs itself" *How to make your business run without You*

"You've got to plan the work and work the plan"

Susan Cater offers the following advice "Write down the steps and procedures to accomplish each task associated with the job."

Systems create leverage. They allow you to control your business and not it control you. They give you consistent levels of service every time. This creates a business that run itself.

"If you can't describe what you are doing as a process, you don't know what you're doing." W. Edwards Deming

Success is not inherent in the act of franchising the business, but rather in the formula owners use in organizing and operating the business as a turnkey system. And the power of this franchise formula can be applied to any business anytime, anywhere to achieve maximum productivity and profitability.

One of the keys to success in business is the development of systems. All great businesses have systems. Systems tell an employee what to do.

Action Item

Write down all the task that you can delegate outside each one write down who will this job be delegated to.

Write down its importance.

Write down how many hours these jobs take.

Now write down the necessity of these jobs.

Now write down the amount of money the person makes who will now do this job.

How much money can you save by delegating or better yet how much is it costing you if you continue to do it.

What systems will you create first?

Dedicate at least 2-3 hours a week and start working on creating systems?

Put it on calendar. Block the time out.

Break into smaller chunks if need be.

Think through the way you currently do things. Is there a better, cheaper, quicker way?

Do you need to create checklists, flowcharts?

Can someone by looking at your systems tell how things should be done from start to finish. Get feedback.

Tweak systems as needed.

Will your business ever be more than it is?

What is keeping you from taking action? You know what you should be doing so why aren't you doing it. Do you expect business success to just happen because you deserve it? Well chances are high it won't. You've got to work at it consistently over and over. Your business will only get better if you get better.

If you are only experiencing a small amount of success or a few clients, then its' time to examine your daily habits to see what you are doing to take your business to next level. A business coach (specializing in small business) can prove to be very beneficial. A business coach can often help you catapult your success (business) to next level in a short period of time. A business coach is often a sounding board, an accountability partner, a cheerleader someone committed to your success. A business coaches main goal is to help you to be successful. This happens because they provide expertise in areas you are struggling with. They often can help you figure out what is holding you back. They can suggest small incremental changes that can make a big difference.

How to avoid making these serious small business mistakes?

Business mistakes-we all make them. Business owners should avoid as many business mistakes as possible by learning from the mistakes of other business owners. Business mistakes could eat all of your time and money very quickly. While making business mistakes are a part of being in business, they should be minimized at all costs.

1. Overworked and underpaid. No time. Frustrated, don't know what to do. Don't know why things aren't working. The first thing you need o do is hire an assistant on-site or a virtual assistant. You can spend a minimal amount and drastically increase productivity and this frees you to do high priority tasks within your business.

2. No money. Most business owners like most Americans are 1 paycheck away from going out of business. They don't know how much cash they have because they don't pay attention to their cash flow. They don't market. They do too many of the wrong things that should be delegated such as those routine tasks that need to be done daily. When a business has very low cash flow he or she must take massive action to get their business back on track.

3. Marketing is not working. The reason it's not working is first you are not measuring it and second you are not appealing to the pain of that customer. Also Marketing should be done in campaigns. It is long term. It is consistent. This is the only way to keep the pipeline full.

4. No direction. Scattered! Working on a zillion things each day but never really accomplishing anything. Entrepreneurs are notorious for this because they are always full of ideas constantly and they are always working on all of them at once instead of focusing on one of them at a time. Focus. Focus. Focus on one thing until it is done and only then move on to something else.

Who doesn't want their business to be a success? Everyone who is in business wants to be successful. So if this is true then why do so many business owners fail each year. While they are obviously numerous variables to consider, most have neglected a few key things to business success. Business Success doesn't come easy. It takes a lot of hard work as well as a plan of action. Business owners who do well, constantly do things they don't want to do. They stay focused on the task at hand despite the distractions they face on the daily basis.

Test everything on your website. Yes, test everything. You will be surprised that small incremental changes can add up to big increases. Often these changes might not make sense to you but they add serious dollars to the bottom line.

Test one part of direct mail piece at a time. Test teasers, colors, and sizes of the envelope and see what gets the best response. Don't be afraid to take a chance, you might be surprised at the results.

Business systems not only create an organized way of doing things, but it also gives your customers a sense of reliability. They know that you are consistent in your actions and more than likely you will do what you say. Do you have a system? Can your business run without you?

Follow Up! Follow up! Follow Up! According to research 80% of sales are lost due to lack of follow up. No small business owner can afford to lose 80% of their sales and continue to be a success. If your sales are low check your follow up process. What happens after the first ad is run or the first direct mail piece goes out or after that networking event that you got 20 business cards from.

Outsource what you don't do well. Delegate things on your to-do list to a virtual assistant or someone else. This will give you the opportunity to focus on the most important things. You will never achieve substantial growth if you don't delegate low priority tasks to someone else.

Always work from a list. Do the most important thing first. Stop doing low priority task that it doesn't matter one way or another whether they get done or not.

Let someone else check your email and take your calls. If you are answering your own calls you are missing out on a lot of money. The reason being these calls distract and disrupt your day when you need to be working on high priority task.

Never stop learning. Attend conferences, webinars, and association meetings often. Not only is this a great opportunity to form alliances, joint ventures and bartering but it allows you to stay sharp and to see emerging trends. Continuous learning is so important especially to the small business owner. "Brian Tracy has shown through studies that each dollar spent on training appropriate employees in the business and corporate world, has brought back 15 to 25 dollars by increased sales, production or performance."

Diversify offerings. Every business should have multiple streams of income especially a service business. Let's face it, if you document how products and services sell during the year, you will quickly see that some products or services sell better than others during certain times of the year. If you only offer one product or service, consider developing more at different price points.

How to improve your business

If you are experiencing subpar success in your business, then you should look at your plan (if you have one). If you don't have one, then a business plan, marketing strategy and business strategy then this should be your 1st step. If you have done the previous, create an ideal client profile.

Learn all you can about your target market.

What about my thinking needs changing?

Consider whether your work is below average. What do your customers have to say about you? Do you have raving customers? What is the 1st impression your potential clients have of you? Do you prospective customers see the value you offer? How are you different?

Determine who your top 5 competitors are. What are their strengths and weaknesses? How much of the market do they control? How can you improve on what they are doing? What is their pricing structure?

Are you at risk of business failure?

Businesses are failing at an alarming rate. Are you in danger of business failure? Below you will find tips on examining a business failure, and how you can turn it around.

If you are working on low value tasks, then chances are you won't be in business long.

Being a business owner or a success at something for that matter requires massive action. A business owner should develop a road map of what needs to be done and by when. And then work that plan tweaking it as needed. If day after day you are doing nothing to grow your business, then chances are you will be out of business soon.

Sometimes business owners are living in a fantasy land when they first go into business thinking that people will automatically knock down their door to buy from them. In reality nothing happens until you market your business and prospects have to see you over and over and then they will start to like, trust and then buy from you.

It takes 7 to 10 contacts before someone even notices you.

If you are working more than 40 hours a week in your business, you will quickly get burn out. Even if you don't your business will lose momentum and you will not work to its full potential because you will be exhausted. Learn to take time off completely from your business at least 1 full day a week to recuperate and you will come back refreshed.

Every business owner goes through this but it should be done to grow the business and to keep up with the current work load. Consider delegating or hiring someone part time to do these tasks.

You will encounter employees who don't care or inadequate. Hire the best staff you can afford. They are a reflection of you and your business. Front line staff are sometimes the 1st and sometimes only face of your business. Invest in Training and educating people on how to treat your customers.

Lack of training. Business Owners cannot assume that staff know what to do and how to do it just because it makes sense to you. Training is worth the investment as it will return to you at least several dollars in return for your investment.

I recently visited a business whose staff could use some training in customer service and sales to say the least. If your sales are low and you are getting some traffic (a fair amount of traffic, it's time to do some training).

Use Traffic stats. The use of some type of Analytics Software such as Google Analytics is helpful in seeing where traffic is coming from. This analytical software can also provide information such as keywords prospects are typing in to get to your site, pages visited, estimated time spent on each page. This provides key information in making decisions for your business.

Training is as important to a small business as it is to a big one. The returns are major. Don't worry, if they leave after receiving this training. You should be more concerned with the effects if you don't do the training at all.

Ignoring cash flow or lack thereof. Knowing how much cash you have coming in and going out is essential for staying afloat. Without the information, you will be out of cash before you know it.

Prepare for times when cash flow will be higher than others. They are inevitable. Implement strategies to constantly keep sales up. Use upsell and cross sell strategies. Realize that Marketing is an investment not an expense. When things are bad, don't stop Marketing. Reevaluate your business and continue to market.

Not knowing what's working and what's not. Knowing what is working and what is not will help leverage resources. Most business owners waste money weeks sometimes months because they don't take the time to learn and measure the things that are working.

Why Education based Marketing

People don't want to be sold. They want to buy your product or service to solve their problems. How does a prospect feel after coming in contact with you? Do they feel like they have been cheated or taken for a ride? If you are not sure, conduct a survey or consider doing with you do with a prospect with someone you trust. Get them to rate you on several categories and get their honest feedback.

Education based Marketing is so much better than a hard sales pitch. We live in an information world but not all of that information is easy to find nor is it easy to understand. Education Based Marketing provides information in a unique fashion often hitting pain points the client is facing and how they can be solved. Education based Marketing can shed light on trends, mistakes, challenges, issues, statistics on things relevant to the prospect. It puts a spin on the normal sales process from with. Education Based Marketing customers see a change is necessary and consequences of not changing.

Marketing message has to be all about the client/customer not you.

Do you have the following sales tools? Are they focused on you or the client?

Business Pen

Business Card

List of questions to find out more about company

Qualifying Questions

Profit

"Life Gives Us Exactly What We Expect?

"The belief that dreams are impossible to achieve prevents most people from getting what they want. Their experience certainly seems to support this belief. They get exactly what they expect from life: boredom, frustration, obstacles, and small incomes. People are what they believe themselves to be, no more, no less." "How to think like a millionaire Mark Fisher

"A goal that is not written down is a wish."

"Understand/Listen to the problems of your customers." Always look for Win Win Solutions

Goals

Write goals out daily.

Visualize them achieved. Visualize the end result.

Change habits.

Do the most important things 1st each day.

Stop saying what you are going to do and do it.

Delegate

Best Practices

Get rid of the clutter.

Be positive

Surround yourself with people who are better than you. Surround yourself with winners. Who are 10 people who are around you most? Include as many non-family members as possible. Because you can't get rid of family

Pay attention to what you do daily. How much time are you wasting each day?

Treat people right.

Expect to increase sales

Build relationships

Ask for referrals

Prioritize

Do ten things a day to get business.

Become known as an expert

What are you trying to get your customers to buy?

What problems will this product or service solve?

How long will it take to solve these problems?

Social Media

Social Media Strategy

Groupon

Twitter

Facebook

LinkedIn

Blogging

Joint Ventures

Strategic Alliance

Marketing

Is there a mini niche?

How will you increase profits? What method will you use? Who is your target market? What need are you filling? What problems do they have? What is the competition doing?

How can you maximize the earning potential? Can you provide more at a greater value?

How much does it cost on the front end to get customer? How much will you make over the life of the customer? How much on the back end?

Multiple Streams of Income

What streams of Income can you produce?

Mastermind Group

Join a Mastermind Group. If you can't find one, create one.

While you are waiting on new clients, this is preparation time. Spend this time wisely.

Referral Strategy

Sales Process

Time Management

Search Engine Optimization

Title tags

Metatags

Keywords

Heading 1

Heading 2

Heading 3

Article Marketing

Write articles that will help you clients/customers in using your products. Educate them on how it will make their lives more convenient, better, bigger or more profitable.

Link Building

Write a book/white paper/audio on improving/myths/mistakes/secrets/tips

Take Action

No matter your intentions nothing really matters until you take massive action. It is my opinion if you don't have enough clients or customers you have even more time to do what needs to be done to grow your business. You can say I don't know what to do or whether I should do this or do that, the truth is no one really knows until they try it, yes try everything and test and see where you get the results. Then do more of what you see getting results.

If you don't have a website, get one.

Get prepared!

What if you get 100 or 1000 new clients today? Could you handle it? My guess is probably not. So you have to get ready.

Need help but can't afford it! Hire someone on Upwork or Guru for cheap. Just be sure to check the ratings or feedback before you give your hard earned money to someone.

Charity

This is twofold. Give to those who are less fortunate.

Give to someone a free service or a free product. "Help enough people get what they want and you will get what you want."

Open your mouth and tell everyone you meet what you do. Be prepared. Give out your cards everywhere. Go to where your customers are at least weekly, daily if you want to see massive results.

This is a side note but a great one I might add. "The average person has four ideas a year which, if anyone is acted on, would make them a millionaire." Brian Tracy, author and motivational speaker

Select someone in your field either local or national who is successful and watch to see how they get clients in the form of Marketing. Do what they do!

Who are the top 10 successful people in your industry? What do they do as far as getting clients?

1. _____

2. _____

3. _____

4. _____

5. _____

6. _____

7. _____

8. _____

9. _____

10. _____

Resources

How did you hear about us form? Put this form by register or phone (You can use the tally marks). Also use with your web site analytics and when someone buys something. If you do free consults or free coaching calls, ask them as well.

Advertisement

Website

Search Engine

Referral (Name of person or company should be on another form)

Direct Mail

Ad

Social Media

Facebook

Twitter

Linked in

Article

Squidoo

Write 1 article a day. At the end of the week, have a VA submit to ezinearticles.com.

About the Author

Shonda Miles has been self-employed for 18 years. She has owned businesses ranging from an online retail store to a Training Company.

Shonda Miles is the CEO of Shonda Miles International, a company helping organizations and individuals improve performance and achieve their goals. Shonda Miles is here to help you achieve your full potential. Her purpose is to help millions of people achieve their goals and live their God given talent.

Shonda Miles is an Author, Entrepreneur, Speaker, Personal Development Trainer, Business Consultant and Business Coach. She loves reading Nonfiction books, writing business books and shopping. Personal Development is her mission. Shonda speaks, blogs and writes about a variety of personal development topics such as Time Management, Success, Goal Setting and having a Positive Attitude.

Shonda's goal is to help others achieve the level of success they desire.

Shonda Miles is a MBA Graduate. She has several successful businesses.

Shonda Miles can be reached at info@shondamiles.com or via her website at www.shondamiles.com.

www.ingramcontent.com/pod-product-compliance
Lightning Source LLC
Chambersburg PA
CBHW070330190526
45169CB00005B/1821